To Henry, Fulton, Pio, Fred, Helen, and Julia.
Shine your Light, be light to each other!

- C.H.

To Nicolas, Elijah, Sarah, Luke, Matthias, and Jude.
Always follow the light of Christ.

- T.D.

Published by Word on Fire Spark, an imprint of
Word on Fire, Park Ridge, IL 60068
Printed in the United States of America
In collaboration with Likable Art and Providential Co.

ISBN: 978-1-68578-029-6

Printed in United States

Second edition.

These supporters helped get this book off the ground.
Thank you for your generosity!

Theresa Clark
Mary Kate Elfelt
Jordan and Annette Robbins
Isaias and Sarah Santillano
Mary Beth Szczepaniak
Brandon Vogt

Special thanks to our editors:
Marie Heimann, Andy Bonjour, Jessie Leatherby, Mark Guiney, Rachel Segura, and Erica Faunce

Follow us at:
wordonfire.org
@wordonfire

lightofthesaints.com
@lightofthesaints

A SHINE the LIGHT BOOK

LIGHT OF THE SAINTS

WORDS BY
Cory Heimann

PICTURES BY
Tricia Dugat

GO GET YOUR FLASHLIGHT!
IT'S TIME FOR A LOOK!

A bunch of God's heroes are right in this book.

If you're deep in the dark, feeling lost in the night,

And you wish – oh you wish! – for just one little light,

Don't worry or scurry or mumble or groan.

Have hope and remember, you're never alone.

SHINE THE LIGHT
BEHIND THE PAGES
WITH THIS SYMBOL
IN THE CORNER!

Try it on the previous page!

Juan Diego was climbing a wintery hill,
When Our Lady in blue said, "Juancito, be still.
I'm Mary, your Mother, tell the Bishop I'm here.
Fill your cloak with my flowers, and have no more fear."
When Juan poured the roses out onto the dirt,
an image of Mary appeared on his shirt.

SAINT JUAN DIEGO, MEXICO

BE FAITHFUL
LIKE JUAN DIEGO.

The candles were taken, but Heaven shined bright.
No bandit could steal God's glorious light.
Despite being young, Anna led them in prayer,
Guiding these martyrs to Heaven with care.

BE PRAYERFUL
LIKE ANNA.

From high on a mountain, in a fine Polish breeze,
Came John Paul the Second, the pope on two skis!
"Don't worry", he said, "don't fear and don't hide.
The darkness is big, but the light is inside.
Paddle all streams, climb high, wander far.
Spreading the light wherever you are."

SAINT JOHN PAUL II, POLAND

BE HOPEFUL
LIKE JOHN PAUL.

Veronica watched as Christ carried His cross,
The wooden beam heavy, his strength almost lost.
With her empty cloth, she wiped off His face,
And the image of Jesus showed up in its place.

BE GENTLE
LIKE VERONICA.

Martin De Porres cut hair in Peru.
Cutting hair is something that you could do too.
And maybe, like him you could fly in the sky,
Or bilocate through prayer if you gave it a try.

SAINT MARTIN DE PORRES, PERU

BE KIND
LIKE MARTIN.

At the top of a hill, in a little stone town,
Padre Pio would listen, beard white, habit brown,
To the next one in line, who had waited so long,
"Oh Padre," they'd say. "I've done so much wrong."
But Jesus forgave every sin, for he knew
Our wounds are a way that the light can shine through.

SAINT PADRE PIO, ITALY

BE WISE
LIKE PIO.

Charbel the Hermit would pray through the night,
Using his lantern to give him some light.
One night, a trick on his lantern was played
Swapping oil with water, but it still displayed
A miraculous light, and what do you know!
This Saint kept on praying, the lamp kept its glow.

SAINT CHARBEL MAKHLOUF, LEBANON

The scars on her body showed she was mistreated,
But this woman, Josephine, wasn't defeated.
From darkness that ruled her life as a slave,
She found healing light from the One we all crave.

SAINT JOSEPHINE BAKHITA, SUDAN

Mary followed Christ Jesus to every new place
And witnessed how freely He poured out His grace.
She thought He was gone, but the angel corrected,
"He's no longer dead, He's been Resurrected!"

BE JOYFUL
LIKE MARY.

In his poncho and hat, this cowboy was tough.
He helped a poor village have more than enough.
This priest hopped from his mule, a shovel in hand.
"Come, friends," José said, "Let's make this place grand!"

SAINT JOSÉ BROCHERO, ARGENTINA

BE LOVING
LIKE JOSÉ.

Once upon a time, but not long ago
Lived a doctor, Gianna, who let a life grow.
Her baby was born, and others would know
The sacrifice only a mother can show.

BE GENEROUS
LIKE GIANNA.

So never be fearful. Don't cower or hide.
For Jesus, your own little light, lives inside.
He'll never go out and His love never ends.
You carry His light, like your many Saint friends
Who found Him inside, even when it was night.
He's calling you, too, to be one little light.

THE END.